THE AUSSIE ABC

WRITTEN BY KIRSTIE HIRST & JADE TONKIN
ILLUSTRATED BY JADE TONKIN

The Aussie ABC

Copyright © Kirstie Hirst and Jade Tonkin 2023

The Author has asserted their rights under the Copyright Act 1968 (the Act) to be identified as the author of this work.

All rights reserved. No part of this publication may be reproduced, stored in a retrieval system, or transmitted in any form or by any means, electronic, mechanical, photocopying, recording or otherwise, without the prior written permission of the author. Any person who does any unauthorised act in relation to this publication may be liable to criminal prosecution and civil claims for damages.

The Australian Copyright Act 1968 (the Act) allows a maximum of one chapter or ten per cent of this book, whichever is the greater, to be photocopied for educational purposes by an educational institution holding a statutory education licence provided that the educational institution (or body that administers it) has given a remuneration notice to the Copyright Agency (Australia) under the Act.

ISBN: 978-1-923163-06-5 (Paperback)

A catalogue record for this book is available from the National Library of Australia

Self-Published by Kirstie Hirst and Jade Tonkin with assistance by Clark & Mackay

Proudly printed in Australian by Clark & Mackay

C IS FOR A CURLEW PLAYING A MATCH OF CRICKET

N IS FOR NUMBAT CROSSING THE NULLARBOR

T is for Tasmanian Devil Wearing Thongs

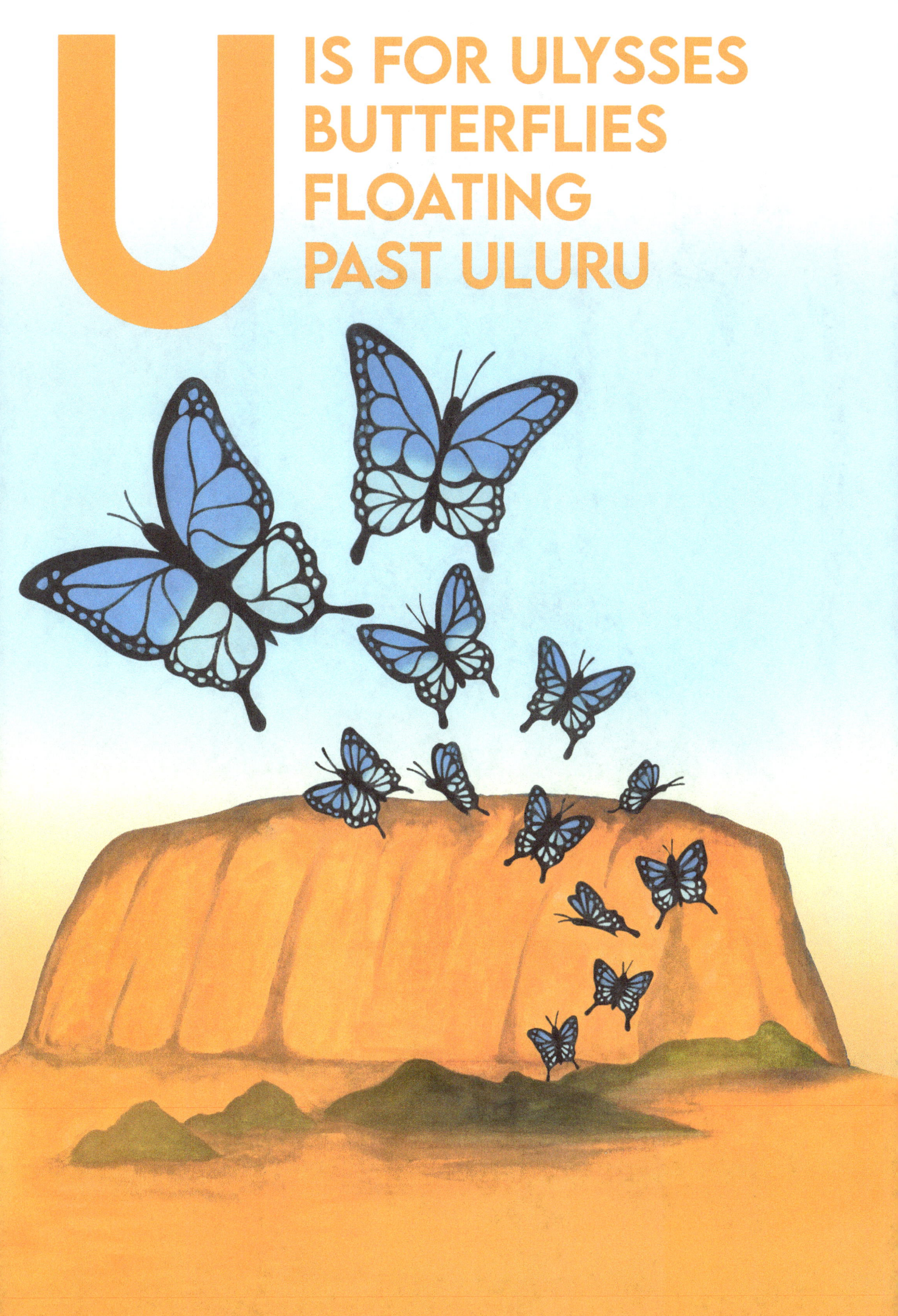

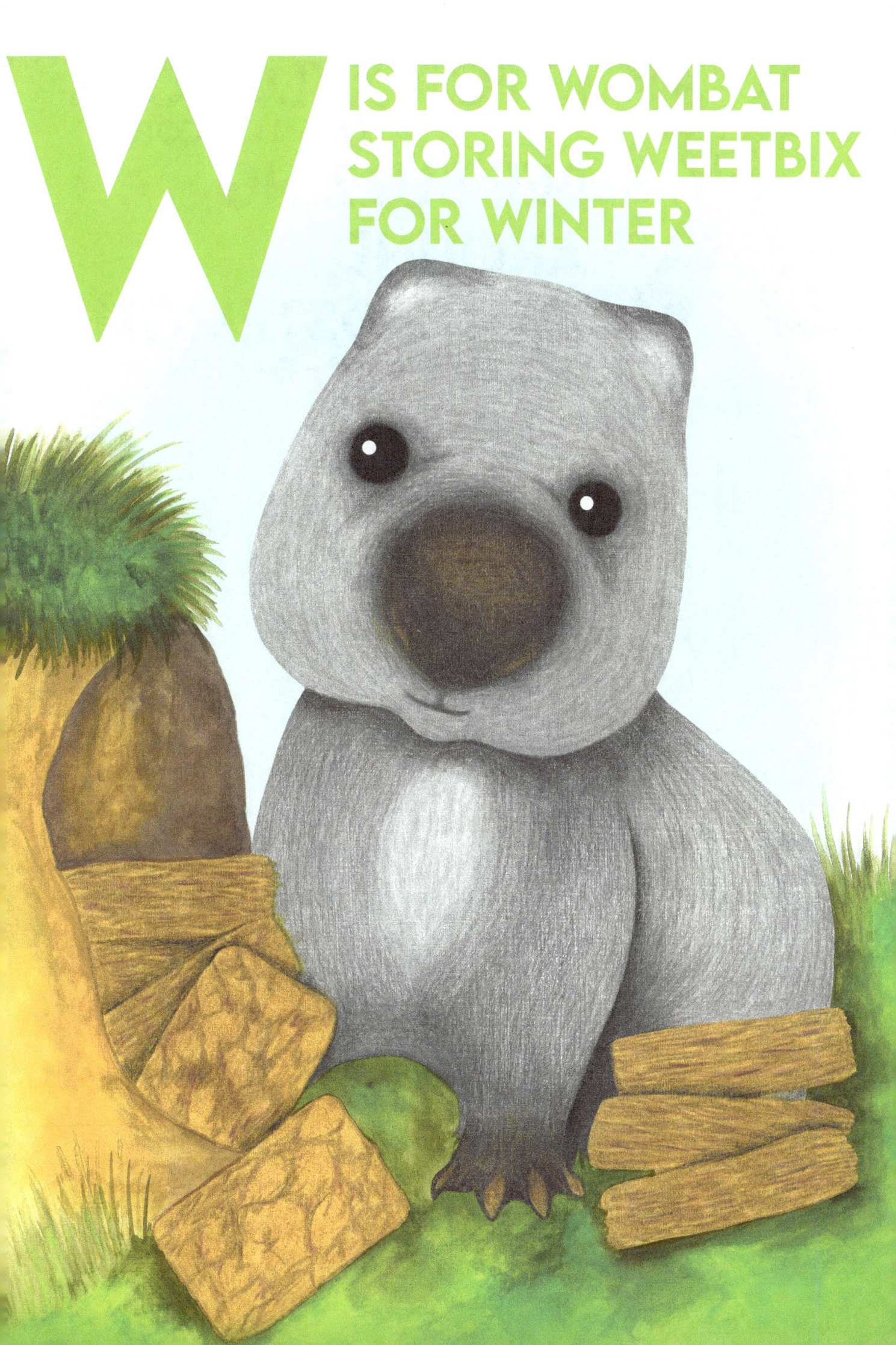

X IS FOR XYLOCOPA
(ZY - LO - COPA)

BEE BUZZING AROUND XANTHOSTEMON
(ZAN - THOST - E - MON)

www.ingramcontent.com/pod-product-compliance
Lightning Source LLC
Chambersburg PA
CBHW081919090526
44591CB00014B/2399